FEB   2012

Countries Around the World
Iraq

Paul Mason

Chicago, Illinois

www.heinemannraintree.com

Visit our website to find out more information about Heinemann-Raintree books.

To order:

☎ Phone 888-454-2279

💻 Visit www.heinemannraintree.com to browse our catalog and order online.

Edited by Louise Galpine
Designed by Richard Parker
Original illustrations © Capstone Library Limited, Ltd.
Illustrated by ODI
Picture research by Mica Brancic
Originated by Capstone Global Library, Ltd.
Printed by China Translation and Printing Company

15 14 13 12 11
10 9 8 7 6 5 4 3 2 1

Library of Congress Cataloging-in-Publication Data
Mason, Paul, 1967-
  Iraq / Paul Mason.
       p. cm.—(Countries around the world)
  Includes bibliographical references and index.
  ISBN 978-1-4329-5209-9 (hc)—ISBN 978-1-4329-5234-1
(pb) 1. Iraq—Juvenile literature. I. Title.
  DS70.62.M37 2012
  956.7—dc22   2010039143

Acknowledgments

The author and publisher are grateful to the following for permission to reproduce copyright material: Alamy pp. 11 (© Peter Jordan), 12 (© Paul David Drabble), 13 (© Jim West), 17 (© Network Photographer), 37, 39 (© dbimages); Corbis p. 35; Corbis pp. 6 (© epa), 15 (Reuters/© Saad Shalash), 16 (Reuters/© Ali Abu Shish), 19 (Reuters/© Thaier al-Sudani), 23, 36 (EPA/© Ali Haider), 24 (Reuters/© Kareem Raheem), 27 (Reuters/© Faleh Kheiber), 29 (© Gianni Dagli Orti), 30 (© Shawn Baldwin), 31 (epa/© Wael Hamzeh), 32 (Reuters/© John Kolesidis), 33 (Reuters/© Mohammed Ameen); Getty Images pp. 5 (Science Faction/Ed Darack), 7 (AFP Photo/ Daniel Mihailescu), 9 (Time Life Pictures); Shutterstock pp. 20 (© Daniel Prudek), 21 (© David Dohnal), 46 (© Iakov Filimonov).

Cover photograph of the ziggurat, Agargouf, Iraq reproduced with permission of Getty Images/Robert Harding World Imagery/Nico Tondini.

We would like to thank Peter Sluglett for his invaluable help in the preparation of this book.

Every effort has been made to contact copyright holders of any material reproduced in this book. Any omissions will be rectified in subsequent printings if notice is given to the publisher.

All the Internet addresses (URLs) given in this book were valid at the time of going to press. However, due to the dynamic nature of the Internet, some addresses may have changed, or sites may have changed or ceased to exist since publication. While the author and publisher regret any inconvenience this may cause readers, no responsibility for any such changes can be accepted by either the author or the publisher.

Contents

Some words are printed in bold, **like this**. You can find out what they mean by looking in the glossary.

Introducing Iraq

Have you seen news of Iraq on TV or in the newspapers? If so, you probably know that Iraq today is trying to rebuild itself. This is necessary because for many years, brutal **dictators** ruled Iraq. Then, in 2003, forces led by the United States, including troops from the United Kingdom, invaded Iraq. This sparked violence that almost tore the country apart.

People of Iraq

Iraqi society is made up of different religious and **ethnic groups**. The main religion is Islam, and about 97 percent of Iraqis are **Muslim**. Islam itself is divided into two main **sects**, or groups.

About 33.5 percent of Iraqis are Sunni Muslims. Most Muslims around the world are also Sunnis. Another 63.5 percent of Iraq's population are Shi'i Muslims. Iran and Lebanon also have large Shi'i populations.

Most Iraqis are **Arabs**. Arabs live throughout the **Middle East** and share many religious and cultural beliefs. Iraq is also home to other ethnic groups. About 17.5 percent of Iraqis are Kurds. Although most Kurds are Sunnis, their strongest links are to other Kurds. Kurds live in northern Iraq, as well as in Iran, Turkey, and Syria.

About 3 percent of Iraqis are neither Shi'i, Sunni, nor Kurd; most of them are Christians.

Daily life

Iraqis usually say hello with a handshake and smile. They say the words "*as-salam alaykum*" (ah-suh-lahm uh-LAY-koom), meaning "peace be with you" in Arabic. Good friends of the same sex may also kiss each other, first on the right cheek, then on the left.

Small villages exist beside the Euphrates River, with the vast Iraqi desert behind them.

History: An Ancient Land

Modern Iraq is descended from one of the oldest cultures in the world. Iraq's territory includes two great rivers, the Euphrates and Tigris. The land near these rivers in lower Iraq is very **fertile**. Five thousand years ago, farmers began selling their extra food at market. This made it possible for the world's first cities to appear, because people could now buy the food they needed, instead of growing it.

Mesopotamia

At the time, the land we call Iraq was known as Mesopotamia. Because city-living Mesopotamians did not have to spend all day farming, they could do all kinds of other things instead. Mesopotamians studied science, mathematics, and astronomy. They wrote **epic** poems, developed the world's first laws, and founded the great city of Babylon.

A fisherman casts his net near Kerbala, south of Baghdad. Iraqis have fished this way for thousands of years.

A woman stands in front of the Kufa **mosque** in the holy city of Najaf. Shi'i Muslims believe this is where Ali became leader of their religion.

The Arab invasion

Iraq has a long history of being invaded. The most important invasion happened in 637 CE. That year, Arabs conquered Iraq, bringing the religion of Islam with them. Twenty-four years after the invasion, a Muslim leader named Ali (see panel below) was murdered in the Iraqi city of Kufa. This event divided Islam into the Shi'i and Sunni sects.

ALI (CA. 599–661 CE)

Ali was the son-in-law and cousin of Muhammad, the **founder** of Islam. After Muhammad's death, there was an argument about who should lead the religion. Those who wanted Ali as leader were horrified when he was **assassinated** in Kufa in 661. The religion divided between Ali's supporters (the Shi'is) and other Muslims (the Sunnis).

Mongols and Ottomans

In 1258, a Mongol leader named Hulagu invaded Iraq and destroyed the city of Baghdad. The Mongols took control of the region. By the 1530s, the area had become part of the Ottoman Empire, which stretched from Greece in the west to Iran in the east. The Ottomans ruled Iraq until they were defeated in World War I. After the war, the British took control of Iraq and other nearby territories.

The creation of modern Iraq

The British created modern Iraq. They drew its borders, disappointing the Kurds who did not get a state of their own. In 1921, the British appointed an Arab prince named Faisal king of Iraq. His family had been useful to the British during the war, but few Iraqis knew who he was. Britain helped govern Iraq until 1932, when the country became independent. For many years afterwards, the British continued to influence Iraqi politics.

Before modern Iraq was created, the country was divided into three provinces.

FAISAL I (1883-1933)

Iraq's first king was Faisal I. During World War I, Faisal had led an Arab revolt in the Hijaz against the Ottoman Empire. For four months in 1920, he was briefly king of Syria before being thrown out by the French. In 1921 the British made him king of Iraq where he ruled until his death in 1933.

The discovery of oil

In the late 1920s, oil was discovered in northern Iraq. Oil was becoming the world's main important source of energy, making Iraq an important place. In the 1960s, the United States, France, and the **Soviet Union**—as well as Britain—began interfering in Iraqi affairs.

By 1945, the dry, dusty landscape of Kirkuk, in northern Iraq, would be filled with people working for Western oil companies.

The fall of Faisal II

Kings governed Iraq until 1958. That year, General Abd al-Karim Qasim led a **coup** against Faisal II, who had been king since 1939. The king and many of his family and supporters were killed.

This was the first of several violent changes of government in Iraq. In 1963, a group of generals overthrew Qasim. In 1968, another coup brought General Ahmad Hasan al-Bakr to power. Meanwhile, Kurds in northern Iraq were trying to achieve self-rule.

Iraq under Saddam

In 1979, Bakr passed leadership of the country to Saddam Hussein. Saddam was a brutal ruler. He was a Sunni, and under his rule Sunnis controlled Iraq. Shi'is, Kurds, and other Iraqis who might oppose Saddam were imprisoned, tortured, or killed. Saddam started a war with Iran, which lasted from 1980 to 1988. The war killed an estimated 700,000 people from both countries combined.

Saddam worked to develop outlawed chemical, biological, and nuclear weapons, called **weapons of mass destruction (WMDs)**. Saddam's forces used chemical weapons, in the form of poisonous gas, against other Iraqis. In 1988, the Iraq army gassed the Kurdish town of Halabja, killing at least 3,000 people.

In 1990, Saddam's armies invaded the neighboring country of Kuwait, which began the Gulf War. The following year, **United Nations** forces defeated the Iraqi army, forcing it to return to Iraq.

SADDAM HUSSEIN (1937–2006)

Saddam Hussein was born in the small Iraqi town of Tikrit. He first became known as the right-hand man of President Hassan al-Bakr. Saddam replaced Bakr in 1979, and remained president until forces led by the United States forced him from power in 2003. He was executed in 2006.

Saddam Hussein in 1982, three years after he became dictator. Saddam would prove to be a cruel ruler, but when this photo was taken, he had good relations with Western powers.

Invasion

After his defeat in Kuwait in 1991, the United Nations ordered Saddam to destroy his WMDs. But by 2002, the U.S. and British governments suspected that Iraq still had WMDs and was a threat to world peace. They led **Coalition** forces into Iraq in March 2003. By April 9, they had captured Baghdad, the capital city. Coalition troops gained control of Iraq, but WMDs were never found.

YOUNG PEOPLE

Before the 2003 invasion, young people met on the streets in the evenings. They could buy *schawarma* sandwiches and ice-cream, play games, or just chat with their friends. After the invasion, being outside became too dangerous, and most young people stayed indoors.

British Soldiers are on patrol searching for explosive devices on a Basra street.

Continuing violence

After the invasion, violence increased in Iraq. There were several reasons for this. First, the U.S. authorities in charge of Iraq had disbanded the army and the police. Without them, it was impossible to keep order. In addition, Shi'i, Sunni, and Kurdish groups all wanted power in the new Iraq. This sometimes spilled over into violence. Finally, Iraqis who resented the invasion, and Muslim terrorists from other countries, attacked Coalition forces. Hundreds of thousands of Iraqis and thousands of Coalition soldiers died.

Early in 2007, the Coalition began sending more troops to Iraq. Security began to improve. There were fewer attacks on mosques and marketplaces. Fewer people were kidnapped and killed. Life slowly began to return to normal.

This Iraqi woman is one of a group of people being sworn in as a US citizen in 2008. The violence has led to many Iraqis leaving in search of better lives in other countries.

Regions and Resources: Dry Plains and Fertile Valleys

Iraq covers about 438,317 square kilometers (169,235 square miles), making it about twice the size of the state of Idaho. It is home to a variety of landscapes, from mountains to dusty plains to marshlands.

Climate

Iraq's climate is very dry. In most of the country, less than 200 millimeters (8 inches) of rain falls each year. Summer temperatures are similar throughout the country—hot! On the hottest days, temperatures can easily top 40°C (104°F). Winters are mild in the south but can be cold in the mountains of the north. Sometimes there is heavy snow. When this melts, it can cause flooding in central Iraq.

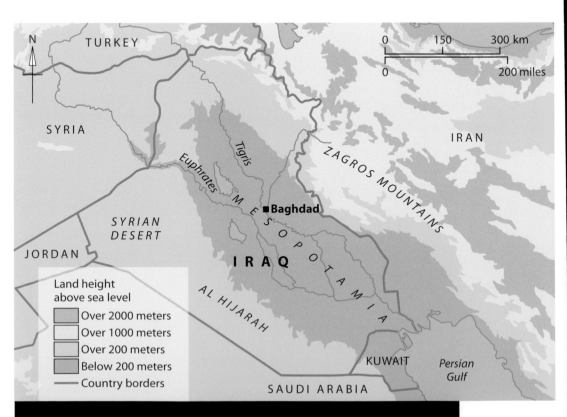

Iraq has a varied landscape that includes such differing areas as mountains, desert land, and marshlands.

All Iraqis dread the arrival of the *shamal*, a hot wind. The *shamal* brings temperatures of well over 40°C (104°F), plus huge sandstorms that can strip the paint from cars.

Major rivers

Iraq has two major rivers, the Tigris and Euphrates, which provide water for almost all the country's agriculture. Both rivers begin in Turkey, flow into Iraq from the north, and end in the south at the Persian Gulf. The two rivers merge at the city of Basra. From Basra to the sea, the great river is known as Shatt al-Arab.

Dry plains

Most of Iraq is made up of dry, flat plains cut by fertile river valleys. West of the Euphrates River these plains turn to desert. There, sandstorms and dust storms regularly send people scurrying indoors for shelter.

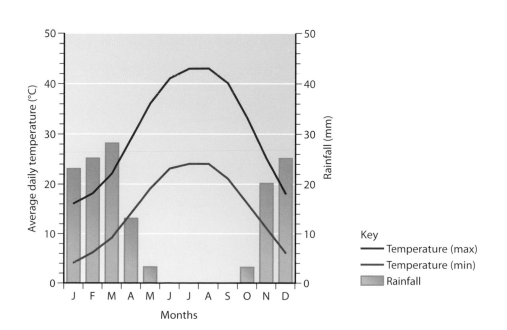

Key
— Temperature (max)
— Temperature (min)
▓ Rainfall

Northern mountains

Heading north from Iraq's plains, travelers climb to a land of high **plateaus** and rolling **steppes**. As they get closer to the northern border, the landscape becomes increasingly mountainous. Some of the peaks reach 4,000 meters (13,000 feet). Temperatures are much cooler than farther south.

Southern marshlands

Large areas of marshland once covered parts of southern Iraq, near the border with Iran. Today, many of these marshlands have been drained so that the water can be used for agriculture or industry. As a result, most of the Marsh Arabs, a **minority** group in Iraq, have lost their homes.

Floods can happen in Iraq when melting snows cause Iraq's river to overflow. Life goes on, though, and people try to carry on with their daily work.

Marsh Arabs, with their distinctive houses made of reeds, once lived throughout southern Iraq. Today, the shrinking of the marshes means their way of life is disappearing.

Seacoasts

Iraq is almost **landlocked**. Its only seacoast is a narrow 58-kilometer (36-mile) strip of coastline between Kuwait and Iran. Basra is Iraq's main port, as well as the capital of Basra, Iraq's southernmost province. Ships that can only travel in deep water cannot use the port of Basra. These have to call at Iraq's other major port, Umm Qasr. This is right beside the border with Kuwait. Umm Qasr was built so that Iraqi ships would not have to travel on the Shatt al-Arab, an area that both Iraq and Iran have claimed.

How to say...

Two phrases that a lost traveler in Iraq might find useful are:

"Ada'tu tareeqi!" ("I'm lost!")
"Hal beemkanek mosa'adati?" ("Can you help me?")

Agriculture

Because Iraq is so dry, only land near rivers can be used for growing food. Most cropland has to be **irrigated**. More than 90 percent of Iraq's water supply is used for agriculture.

The wars and violence of recent years have damaged Iraq's farming industry. For example, Iraq was once one of the biggest producers of fragrant rice in the world. Today, it has to **import** much of the rice its people eat. The same is true of wheat, fruit, and vegetables.

Many Iraqi farmers keep animals, in particular cattle, sheep, and goats. People also keep chickens, which provide them with both eggs and meat.

Daily life

Rice is one of the most popular foods in Iraq. The country's sweet-smelling rice is famous throughout the Middle East. Farmers plant the seedlings by hand in June and July and then keep the crops watered through the hot summer months. By October, the rice is ready to be harvested by hand.

Oil

Iraq's most important industry is oil. It lies underground around the Kurdish regions of the north and in the south near the Kuwaiti border. Oil is extremely valuable, because much of the world relies on it for energy. Oil provides power for motor vehicles, trains, ships, and aircraft. It is also used to manufacture plastics and chemicals. No one is sure how much oil Iraq has, but it probably contains at least the world's fourth-largest reserves. Money from oil could make Iraq a wealthy nation.

This U.S. soldier is standing guard outside an oil refinery in northern Iraq. Oil is Iraq's most important **resource**.

Wildlife: Nature Under Threat

Iraq is home to a diverse selection of birds, reptiles, and mammals. Common animals in Iraq include camels, foxes, gazelles, jackals, and wild pigs. In the marshlands, there is a wide variety of birds, including ducks, herons, and many birds of prey. Visitors to the marshes will also see water buffalo, though these are kept as domestic animals and are not wild.

Wetlands and water shortages

Iraq's wetlands are home to its most varied wildlife, but today they are under threat. When the Marsh Arabs rebelled against Saddam Hussein in 1991, the government cut off supplies of water to the marshes south of Baghdad. The marshlands shrank to roughly one-tenth of their previous size.

Water shortages have also been created because both Syria and Turkey have built dams across the Euphrates. These dams take water from the river before it reaches Iraq.

Iraq's waterways and wetlands make the country an excellent habitat for water birds such as the stiff-tailed white duck.

Iraq is home to large birds of prey including the honey buzzard. Honey buzzards eat mainly insects, especially wasps and hornets, but will also eat mice, lizards, snakes, and small birds.

Wildlife conservation

Years of conflict have also harmed Iraq's wildlife. Oil has leaked into the environment, particularly waterways, from damaged pipelines and oil wells. The oil coats plants, birds, and animals, and kills thousands each year.

Iraq was once home to the Asiatic lion, Asiatic cheetah, and Caspian tiger. These species have now disappeared from the country (and the Caspian Tiger has been hunted to extinction everywhere).

Daily life

Many Iraqi rivers ran dry in the summer of 2009. The snakes of the marshes and riverbanks began to head for nearby towns, looking for food. Many were poisonous, so people had to keep a careful watch for snakes wherever they went.

Infrastructure: A Changing Country

Iraq is changing. It has slowly been rebuilding its government and **infrastructure** after years of war and dictatorships.

Government and politics

Iraq has a **federal** government. The country is divided into 18 provinces and 1 region. Under the 2005 **constitution**, the provinces elect representatives, who join the 325-member Council of Representatives. The Council of Representatives chooses the prime minister and the government. Eight seats on the council are reserved for Iraq's minorities, such as Christians. Iraq also has a president.

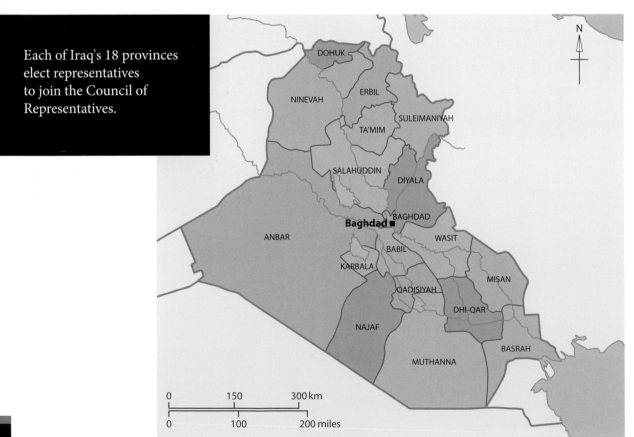

Each of Iraq's 18 provinces elect representatives to join the Council of Representatives.

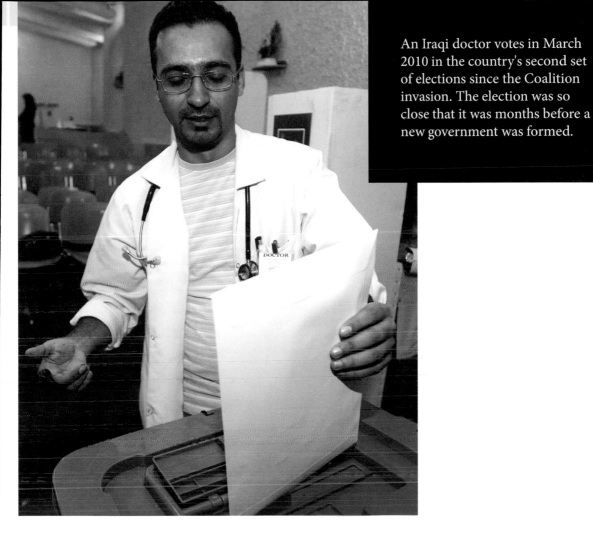

An Iraqi doctor votes in March 2010 in the country's second set of elections since the Coalition invasion. The election was so close that it was months before a new government was formed.

There are many political parties in Iraq. They are usually based on religious or ethnic identity: most are Shi'i, Sunni, or Kurdish. Together, the Shi'i parties make up the largest group, but the balancing force of the Kurds and Sunnis makes it hard for any one group to dominate.

JALAL TALABANI (1933–)

Jalal Talabani is a Kurd. In 1961 and again in 1974-75, he took part in Kurdish rebellions against the Iraqi government. When Coalition forces invaded Iraq in 2003, Talabani helped organize Kurdish forces in the north. He was appointed president in 2005 and was then elected to the same post by Iraqis in 2006.

Iraqi girls listen to their teacher on the first day of the school year in September 2005. Girls and boys are almost always taught in separate classes in Iraq.

Education

Iraqis once had one of the best education systems in the Middle East. This is no longer the case. After the Gulf War ended in 1991, Iraq could not afford teachers, schools, and supplies. Then, after Coalition forces invaded Iraq in 2003, few children were able to attend school regularly. The streets were too violent for them to go to school.

YOUNG PEOPLE

Many schoolchildren wear uniforms to school, especially in Iraq's cities. Typically, girls wear long, dark dresses, and a white long-sleeved top. Most also wear a headscarf. Boys wear dark trousers and a polo shirt.

War destroyed many of Iraq's schools. Those schools that remain often have too many students. To fit everyone in, the students may be split into groups. The first group arrives early in the morning and has a few hours of lessons. They leave to make space for a second group. In areas where few schools are still standing, there may even be a third group of students later in the day.

Boys and girls

In Iraq today, 84 percent of males and 64 percent of females aged 15 and older can read. Fewer women can read and write because some Iraqis think that education is not as important for girls as for boys. They think a woman's job is to be a wife and mother, and that for this she will need other skills. As a result, boys stay in school an average of eleven years, while girls leave after an average of eight.

Health care

Health care in Iraq is free, but the health care system is troubled because of the violence. After the Gulf War, the Iraqi government ran out of money to pay for hospitals, equipment, and doctors. Then, after the 2003 invasion, the hospitals that remained standing often had no medicines, and sometimes no electricity.

Iraq also has a shortage of doctors. Many doctors left the country following the invasion by Coalition forces in 2003. Some reports say that half of Iraq's doctors left the country.

For many years, Saddam's policies and international **sanctions** trying to force change hurt Iraqis. People found it hard to get enough to eat. In 2003, things got worse when clean water became scarce and **sewage** systems were destroyed. Disease became more common.

How to say...

Do you speak Arabic? If not, here are some phrases that might be useful in Iraq:

Ma-atakallam arabi   "I don't speak Arabic"
Titkallam inglizi?   "Do you speak English?"

Improvements

Today, the health care system in Iraq is slowly improving. Hospitals have more supplies, and local clinics have opened. Many children have been **vaccinated** against diseases, food is generally more plentiful, and water supplies are improving.

In 2006 vaccinations for diseases such as polio were available for the first time in years. In Baghdad, mothers lined up to register their children for vaccinations.

YOUNG PEOPLE

Most Iraqi teenagers today spent their childhoods feeling hungry. In the years after Iraq's 1991 defeat in the Gulf War, food was often in short supply. Up to one in ten children had health problems as a result of not getting enough food.

Culture: Ancient and Modern

People have lived in what is now Iraq for more than 5,000 years. Ancient Iraqi culture produced many remarkable works. But Iraq also has a vibrant modern culture, with music, film, and sports all playing an important part in the life of the country.

Ancient treasures

Iraq's museums contain statues, jars, and other treasures from Mesopotamia that are thousands of years old. After Coalition forces invaded in 2003, many museums were **looted**, and many ancient treasures were stolen. Some **artifacts** have been recovered, but others may never be found. Many important pieces disappeared from the National Museum of Iraq in Baghdad, which remained closed in 2010.

National anthem

In 2003, Iraqis decided their old national anthem was too closely linked to Saddam Hussein's brutal rule. Its new anthem, from a poem called "Mawtini" ("My Homeland," in Arabic), was written by Ibrahim Touqan in about 1934. It begins:

> *My homeland, My homeland*
> *Glory and beauty, Sublimity and splendor*
> *Are in your hills, Are in your hills*
>
> *Life and deliverance, Pleasure and hope*
> *Are in your air, Are in your Air*
> *Will I see you? Will I see you?*
> *Safe and comforted, Sound and honored.*

This carving is from the throne of Shalmaneser III, who ruled what is now Iraq between 859 BCE and 824 BCE.

GERTRUDE BELL (1868–1926)

Gertrude Bell was an English writer, **archaeologist**, and **diplomat** fascinated by the Middle East. She played an important role in creating modern Iraq in 1921, and she founded the Iraqi National Museum in Baghdad. The museum opened in 1926, shortly before her death.

Music

Iraq's traditional music usually features a guitarlike instrument called an *oud*. It has a bowl-shaped back and a short neck. In Iraq, the *oud* typically has 13 strings, but *ouds* from other countries typically have 11.

Poetry is very popular in Iraq, and performances are often set to traditional music. Today, many of Iraq's most popular musicians blend traditional and modern instruments.

Some Iraqi musicians make Western-style music, especially rock, hip-hop, and pop. But some religious **extremists** object to the performers and the words of their songs. They are sometimes violent toward people associated with Western-style music.

Naseer Shamma, one of Iraq's most famous *oud* players, performs in Cairo, Egypt, in 2009. The musicians are all playing *ouds* in the picture.

KAZEM AL SAHER (1957–)

Kazem Al Saher is one of the Middle East's most popular musicians. He has been called the "Elvis of the Middle East." Kazem sold his bicycle at age 10 to buy a guitar. He later learned to play the *oud* and became famous across the Arab world as a singer, musician, and poet. He now lives in Cairo, Egypt.

TV and radio

A wide variety of TV channels are available in Iraq. The state broadcaster is called *al Iraqiya*, and there are also many satellite channels. There are Shi'i, Sunni, and Kurdish TV channels.

Iraqis can choose from a huge number of radio stations. There are stations that give news, play music, host debates, and broadcast religious messages. Most stations are in Arabic, but Kurdish, English, and other languages can also be heard.

Sports

Iraqis love sports. All around the country, children play basketball on street corners and soccer wherever they can find the space.

Soccer is the most popular sport in Iraq. The country has a professional soccer league, and the national team has done well in the Olympics and the Asian Games in recent years. The Premier League is the top division, and its matches attract big, enthusiastic crowds. Basketball also has a professional league in Iraq.

Wrestling

Wrestling is popular in Iraq, as it has been throughout the Middle East for hundreds of years. Recently, judo has also become popular. In 2008, Riyadh Al Azzawi became the first Iraqi world champion at kickboxing. Al Azzawi is based in London, England and he has also been British and European champion, but that did not stop Iraqis from celebrating his win!

Iraqi player Hawar Mulla Mohammed shields the ball during a match at the 2004 Olympic Games. The Iraqi team reached the semi-finals.

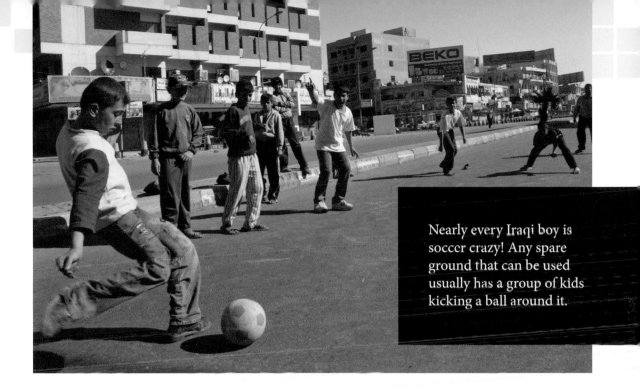

Nearly every Iraqi boy is soccer crazy! Any spare ground that can be used usually has a group of kids kicking a ball around it.

Weightlifting

Another popular sport in Iraq is weight lifting. Abdul Wahid Aziz won a bronze medal in weightlifting at the 1960 Olympics. He was the first—and as of 2010, the only—Iraqi to win an Olympic medal.

How to say...

Here are the names of popular sports in Arabic:

Kurat al-qadam   soccer
Korat salaa   basketball
Kurat al-qadam alamriikiya   American football
Al-baysbuul   baseball
As-sibaaha   swimming

Festivals and holidays

Many of Iraq's festivals are religious. During the month of Ramadan, Muslims **fast** from sunup to sundown to help improve their spiritual lives. Muslims celebrate the end of *Ramadan* with a celebration called *'Id al-Fitr*.

Food

Whenever Iraqis get together, they enjoy sharing food. People eat rice with most meals, and bread is common. Meals often include green beans, okra, eggplant, and tomatoes. Few Iraqis can afford meat except on special occasions. Lamb is the most popular meat.

Adas Bil Hamod recipe

During *Ramadan*, many Iraqis eat food with lentils before dawn. The lentils are digested slowly and provide energy right through to the evening. Ask an adult to help you make this dish of lentils with lemon juice.

Ingredients

- 1½ pounds lentils
- 2 potatoes, peeled and chopped
- 2 tablespoons vegetable oil
- 6 garlic cloves, crushed
- ¼ cup chopped coriander
- 2 tablespoons flour
- 1 tablespoon water
- ¼ cup lemon juice
- Salt and pepper

Instructions

Boil the lentils in a pot of water for 15 minutes. Then add the potatoes, and cook until soft.

Heat the oil in a frying pan, and fry the garlic and coriander until the garlic is soft. Add the garlic and coriander to the lentils and potatoes. In a small bowl, mix the flour and water in to a paste, and then add it to the lentil mixture. Cook for 30 minutes over medium heat.

Before serving, add the lemon juice and a little salt and pepper. Serve hot or cold with pita bread.

Daily life

All Iraqis look forward to public holidays, which usually celebrate religious festivals or important days in Iraq's history.

- January 1: New Year's Day
- January 6: Army Day
- February (exact date varies): Mouloud (Birth of the Prophet Muhammad)
- April 9: Baghdad Liberation Day
- April 17: FAO Day
- May 1: Labor Day
- July 14: Republic Day
- August 8: Ceasefire Day (End of Iran-Iraq War)
- October 3: Iraqi Independence Day (National Day)

A man hands out rice to pilgrims on their way to a religious festival. Hospitality is important to Iraqis.

Daily life

Guests eating at someone's house will always leave a little food on their plate when they have finished. If they don't, their hosts will feel that they are still hungry, and that they have not been able to offer enough food.

Iraq Today

Iraq has known little peace since the Iran-Iraq War began in 1980. In 1990, it attacked Kuwait, and its defeat in 1991 was followed by 12 years of sanctions. The country became poorer, and Saddam Hussein's government became more brutal. Then, in 2003, the invasion by U.S.-led Coalition troops sparked a long wave of violence. What did the future hold for Iraq, after Coalition combat forces left the country in 2010?

Slow improvements

The key to Iraq's future is ending the violence that began after the 2003 invasion. Since 2007, the violence has been decreasing. Iraq's police force has also become more effective. As people had less reason to be afraid, business and social activity in Iraq improved.

An Iraqi woman votes during the 2010 elections. Although security had improved by then, the elections were still affected by violence.

Each year, more Iraqis have access to clean water, electricity, gas, education, and health services. Life is still hard for many, but most people feel positive about the future. In 2007, only 39 percent of people felt that life was quite good or good. By 2009, the figure had risen to 65 percent. Slowly, life seems to be improving in Iraq.

After the 2003 invasion, there were many bombings and shootings at Iraq's markets. It became harder and harder to find food. Today, things have improved, and many Iraqis are hopeful about their future.

How to say...

Here are a few ways to say "good-bye" in Arabic:

Ma'a salama Goodbye
Tosbeho 'ala khair Good night (to a man)
Tosbeheena 'ala khair Good night (to a woman)
Araka fi ma ba'd See you later (to a man)
Araki fi ma bard See you later (to a woman)

Fact File

Official name: Republic of Iraq

Type of government: Parliamentary democracy

Languages: Arabic (official language), Kurdish (official language in Kurdish region), Turkoman, Assyrian, and Armenian

Capital city: Baghdad

Major cities and populations: Baghdad, Mosul, Basra, Sulaymaniyah, Arbil, Kirkuk

Population: 29,671,605 (2010 estimated)

Main religion: Islam

Bordering countries: Kuwait, Saudi Arabia, Jordan, Syria, Turkey, Iran

Total area: 438,317 square kilometers (169,235 square miles)

Major rivers: Tigris and Euphrates

Highest point: Unnamed mountain in northern Iraq, at 3,611 meters (11,847 feet) above sea level

Lowest point: Persian Gulf, sea level

Average Rainfall: 156 millimeters (6.1 inches) per year

Currency: Dinar

Key resources: Petroleum, natural gas, sulphur, phosphates

Imports: Food, medicine, manufactured goods

Exports: Crude oil, other fuels, food, live animals

Main trading partners: United States, Syria, Turkey, India, Italy

Life expectancy: 69 years for men, 72 years for women (2010 estimated)

Literacy rate: 74 percent

Prominent Iraqis: Saddam Hussein, president (1937–2006)
Nuri al-Maliki, prime minister
Jalal Talabani, president

National symbols: Eagle, rose

National anthem: "Mawtini"

These people are swimming in the river in Kurdistan in 2010. This region of Iraq is more peaceful now than it has been for many years.

Timeline

BCE means "before the common era." When this appears after a date it refers to the number of years before the Christian religion began. BCE dates are always counted backward.

CE means "common era." When this appears after a date, it refers to the time after the Christian religion began.

BCE

ca. 3000	Cities develop in Mesopotamia.
331–332	Alexander the Great of Greece conquers Mesopotamia.

CE

637	Arab forces bring Islam to the Iraq region.
661	Ali is assassinated in Kufa, beginning the split between the Shi'i and Sunni sects of Islam.
ca. 762	Baghdad is founded.
1258	Forces of the Mongol leader Hulagu take control of Baghdad.
1534	Turkish forces capture Baghdad.
1914–18	Arab and Kurdish forces fight against the Turks in World War I.
1921	British appoint Prince Faisal of Saudi Arabia as the king of Iraq. Few Iraqis know who Faisal is.
1920s	Oil is discovered in Iraq.
1932	Iraq becomes formally independent.
1958	General Abd al-Karim Qasim seizes power.
1968	Hasan al-Bakr becomes president, and a dictator.
1979	Saddam Hussein becomes president of Iraq.

1980	Iraq invades Iran, starting an eight-year war.
1990	Iraq invades Kuwait.
1991	Iraqi forces are driven from Kuwait by United Nations forces.
1991	The United Nations enacts sanctions against Iraq in an effort to make the country destroy its WMDs.
2003	The United States and the United Kingdom lead an invasion of Iraq to search for WMDs.
2003–07	Violence threatens to run out of control in Iraq, with kidnappings and bomb attacks happening every day.
2008	With the violence dying down, the Iraqi government announces that all foreign forces will leave Iraq by the end of 2011.
2010	It was announced that American combat missions in Iraq would come to an end in 2010.

Glossary

Arab Someone whose ancestors originally came from the Arabian peninsula and who speaks Arabic. Many Arabs follow the Muslim religion and share similar tastes in music, food, and clothing.

archaeologist person who studies the remains of past human societies

artifact items created by humans, usually for a practical purpose

assassinate to murder an important person such as the leader of a country

coalition temporary union of people or groups for a specific purpose, for example, when troops from different countries work together

constitution written document that contains all of the governing principles of a state or country

coup overthrow of a country's government, usually by military force

dictator leader who has complete power and is usually brutal

diplomat person who works to keep good relations between different countries

epic long poem that tells a story

ethnic group people with distinct, shared cultural traditions

extremist someone who behaves in an unreasonable way

fast go without eating

federal related to a form of government in which power is distributed between a central government and local governments

fertile producing good crops

founder person who begins or starts something. For example, a person who starts a stamp-collecting club is its founder.

import bring in from another country to sell

infrastructure the basic systems and structures that a country needs in order to work properly, for example roads, railways, or education

irrigate supply with water

landlocked without access to the sea

looted stolen during a time when the police have lost control

Middle East region covering southwest Asia and northeast Africa

minority people who are outnumbered by other groups in a society or country

mosque building where Muslims worship

Muslim person who follows the religion of Islam

plateau raised flat area of land

resource material that can be used by people

sanction limit on contact and trade with a country to force it to change its policies

sect religious group consisting of members with similar beliefs

sewage human toilet waste

Soviet Union communist country that stretched from eastern Europe across Asia. It broke apart into several smaller countries in 1991.

steppe large, open plain

United Nations association of most of the world's countries, which aims to improve economic, political, and social conditions worldwide

vaccinate give medicine, usually in a shot, to prevent someone from getting a specific disease

weapons of mass destruction (WMD) very powerful chemical, biological, or nuclear weapons

Find Out More

Books

IraqiGirl. *IraqiGirl: Diary of a Teenage Girl in Iraq*. Chicago: Haymarket
   Books, 2009.
A book for teenage readers based on the blog of a teenage girl growing up
in Mosul, Iraq. It deals with family, friendships, and community against a
backdrop of violence, death, and destruction.

King, John. *Iraq Then And Now*. Chicago: Heinemann-Raintree, 2005.
Traces the history of Iraq from its earliest days. Also includes detailed
information on the rise of Saddam, his policies, and the run-up to the
decision to invade Iraq in 2003.

Mason, Paul. *Global Hot Spots: Iraq*. New York: Marshall Cavendish, 2008.
Provides information about Iraqi history, Saddam Hussein, the invasion of Iraq
in 2003, and what has happened since then.

Mason, Paul. *Timelines: The Iraq War*. New York: Scholastic, 2010.
A step-by-step guide to what happened and when in the run-up to the
Coalition invasion of Iraq in 2003, plus detailed information about the
changes that have happened in Iraqi politics and society since then.

DVDs

Half Moon. Directed by Bahman Ghobadi. Strand Releasing, 2006.
The story of Mamo, an old, but legendary, Kurdish singer who lives in Iran. He
is determined to give one last concert in Iraqi Kurdistan before he dies.

Turtles Can Fly. Directed by Bahman Ghobadi. MGM 2005.
Set as the world holds its breath for the 2003 invasion of Iraq, this film tells
the story of 13-year-old "Satellite," a Kurdish orphan who is trying to get a TV
working so that people can hear the news as soon as Saddam is defeated.

Websites

www.britishmuseum.org
At the British Museum's website, you can go on online explorations of many world cultures, including Islamic Middle East.

http://oi.uchicago.edu
You can look inside the collections online at the Oriental Institute of Chicago's website and see artifacts from Mesopotamia.

www.theiraqmuseum.org
The Iraq Museum site, like the museum itself, is a work in progress: some pages are blank. There is good, if limited, information on artifacts from Sumer, Babylon, Assyria, and other ancient Iraqi cultures.

http://mesopotamia.lib.uchicago.edu
This site contains information from the University of Chicago on ancient Mesopotamia, including interactive materials and teaching resources.

Places to Visit

British Museum, London, England
The British Museum has one of the world's foremost collections of Mesopotamian artifacts. Key sections include those on Assyria, Sumer, and Babylon.
www.britishmuseum.org

Oriental Institute of the University of Chicago, Chicago, IL, United States
The Oriental Institute has a renowned collection of art and artifacts from the Middle East, and has a gallery featuring material from Mesopotamia.
http://oi.uchicago.edu/

Topic Tools

You can use these topic tools for your school projects. Trace the flag and map on to a sheet of paper, using the thick black outlines to guide you, then color in your pictures. Make sure you use the right colors for the flag!

The colors in the flag of Iraq represent different ideals. Red is for willingness to shed blood, green for Arab fields, black for battles, and white for purity of motives and deeds. The inscription reads "God is Great."

N

Baghdad

Index

Titles in the series